P9-DHS-532

To Katie and
Julia,

From Sandy D'Antonio

TRADITIONAL SONGS

Old MacDonald Had a Farm

Edited by Ann Owen

Illustrated by Sandra D'Antonio

Music Consultant: Peter Mercer-Taylor, Ph.D.
Associate Professor of Musicology, University of Minnesota,
Minneapolis, Minnesota

Reading Consultant: Susan Kesselring, M.A., Literacy Educator
Rosemount-Apple Valley-Eagan
(Minnesota) School District

PICTURE WINDOW BOOKS
MINNEAPOLIS, MINNESOTA

Traditional Songs series editor: Peggy Henrikson
Page production: The Design Lab
Musical arrangement: Elizabeth Temple
The illustrations in this book were rendered in pen with digital coloring.

PICTURE WINDOW BOOKS
5115 Excelsior Boulevard
Suite 232
Minneapolis, MN 55416
1-877-845-8392
www.picturewindowbooks.com

Copyright © 2003 by Picture Window Books
All rights reserved. No part of this book may be reproduced
without written permission from the publisher. The publisher
takes no responsibility for the use of any of the materials or
methods described in this book, nor for the products thereof.

Printed in the United States of America.
1 2 3 4 5 6 08 07 06 05 04 03

Library of Congress Cataloging-in-Publication Data
Old Macdonald had a farm / edited by Ann Owen ; illustrated by Sandra D'Antonio.
p. cm. — (Traditional songs)
Includes bibliographical references (p.).
Summary: Presents an illustrated version of the traditional song along with some
discussion of its folk origins.
ISBN 1-4048-0152-9 (library binding)
1. Children's songs, English—United States—History and criticism—Juvenile literature.
2. Folk songs, English—United States—History and criticism—Juvenile literature.
[1. Children's songs—Texts. 2. Farm sounds—Songs and music. 3. Songs.]
I. Owen, Ann, 1953- II. D'Antonio, Sandra, ill. III. Series.
ML3551 .O52 2003
782.42162'13'00268—dc21
2002155294

What do you see when you sing a song? Does the music come in colors?

What do you do when you sing a song? Does the melody make you dance?

What do you hear when you sing a song? Do the words tell a story?

Let's explore the sights and sounds of one of our favorite songs.

Listen to the noise on Old MacDonald's farm!

chick-chick

chick-chick

Old MacDonald had a farm,
E-I-E-I-O.
And on that farm he had a cow,
E-I-E-I-O.
With a moo-moo here,
and a moo-moo there,
here a moo, there a moo,
everywhere a moo-moo.
Old MacDonald had a farm,
E-I-E-I-O.

Old MacDonald had a farm,
E-I-E-I-O.
And on that farm he had a pig,
E-I-E-I-O.
With an oink-oink here,
and an oink-oink there,
here an oink, there an oink,
everywhere an oink-oink.
Old MacDonald had a farm,
E-I-E-I-O!

Old MacDonald had a farm,
E-I-E-I-O.
And on that farm he had a duck,
E-I-E-I-O.
With a quack-quack here,
and a quack-quack there,
here a quack, there a quack,
everywhere a quack-quack.
Old MacDonald had a farm,
E-I-E-I-O.

Old MacDonald had a farm, E-I-E-I-O.
And on that farm he had some chickens, E-I-E-I-O.
With a chick-chick here, and a chick-chick there,
here a chick, there a chick, everywhere a chick-chick.
Old MacDonald had a farm, E-I-E-I-O.

Old MacDonald had a farm,
E-I-E-I-O.
And on that farm he had a donkey,
E-I-E-I-O.
With a hee-haw here,
and a hee-haw there,
here a hee, there a haw,
everywhere a hee-haw.
Old MacDonald had a farm,
E-I-E-I-O.

Old MacDonald had a farm,
E-I-E-I-O.
And on that farm he had a horse,
E-I-E-I-O.
With a neigh-neigh here,
and a neigh-neigh there,
here a neigh, there a neigh,
everywhere a neigh-neigh.
Old MacDonald had a farm,
E-I-E-I-O.

Old MacDonald had a farm,
E-I-E-I-O.
And on that farm he had a sheep,
E-I-E-I-O.
With a baa-baa here,
and a baa-baa there,
here a baa, there a baa,
everywhere a baa-baa.
Old MacDonald
had a farm,
E-I-E-I-O.

baa-baa

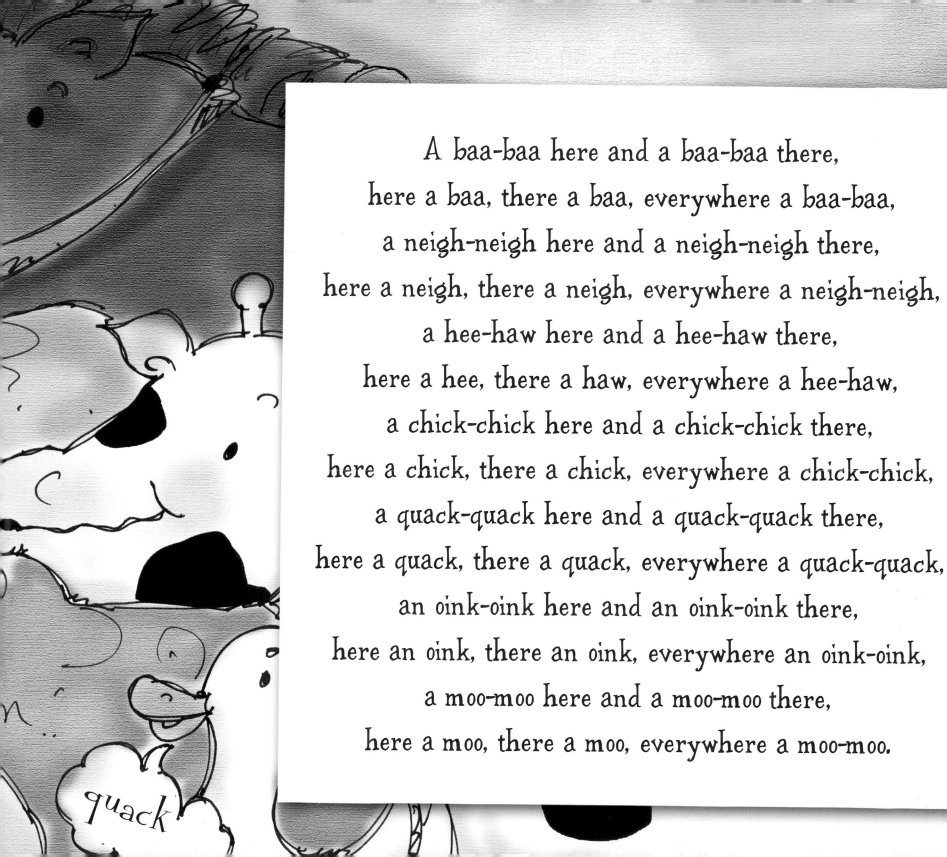

A baa-baa here and a baa-baa there,
here a baa, there a baa, everywhere a baa-baa,
a neigh-neigh here and a neigh-neigh there,
here a neigh, there a neigh, everywhere a neigh-neigh,
a hee-haw here and a hee-haw there,
here a hee, there a haw, everywhere a hee-haw,
a chick-chick here and a chick-chick there,
here a chick, there a chick, everywhere a chick-chick,
a quack-quack here and a quack-quack there,
here a quack, there a quack, everywhere a quack-quack,
an oink-oink here and an oink-oink there,
here an oink, there an oink, everywhere an oink-oink,
a moo-moo here and a moo-moo there,
here a moo, there a moo, everywhere a moo-moo.

quack

Old MacDonald Had a Farm

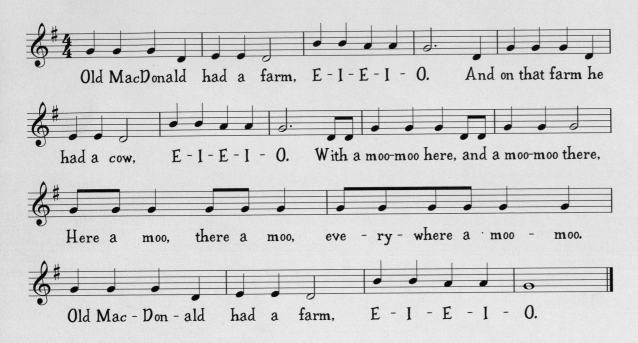

Old MacDonald had a farm, E - I - E - I - O. And on that farm he had a cow, E - I - E - I - O. With a moo-moo here, and a moo-moo there, Here a moo, there a moo, eve - ry - where a moo - moo. Old Mac - Don - ald had a farm, E - I - E - I - O.

Here a quack, there a quack, everywhere a quack-quack,
An oink-oink here, and an oink-oink there,
Here an oink, there an oink, everywhere an oink-oink,
A moo-moo here and a moo-moo there,
Here a moo, there a moo, everywhere a moo-moo.
Old MacDonald had a farm, E-I-E-I-O.

6. Old MacDonald had a farm, E-I-E-I-O.
And on that farm he had a horse, E-I-E-I-O.
With a neigh-neigh here, and a neigh-neigh there,
Here a neigh, there a neigh, everywhere a neigh-neigh,
A hee-haw here, and a hee-haw there,
Here a hee, there a haw, everywhere a hee-haw,
A chick-chick here, and a chick-chick there,
Here a chick, there a chick, everywhere a chick-chick,
A quack-quack here, and a quack-quack there,
Here a quack, there a quack, everywhere a quack-quack,
An oink-oink here, and an oink-oink there,
Here an oink, there an oink, everywhere an oink-oink,
A moo-moo here and a moo-moo there,
Here a moo, there a moo, everywhere a moo-moo.
Old MacDonald had a farm, E-I-E-I-O.

2. Old MacDonald had a farm, E-I-E-I-O.
And on that farm he had a pig, E-I-E-I-O.
With an oink-oink here, and an oink-oink there,
Here an oink, there an oink, everywhere an oink-oink,
A moo-moo here and a moo-moo there,
Here a moo, there a moo, everywhere a moo-moo.
Old MacDonald had a farm, E-I-E-I-O.

3. Old MacDonald had a farm, E-I-E-I-O.
And on that farm he had a duck, E-I-E-I-O.
With a quack-quack here, and a quack-quack there,
Here a quack, there a quack, everywhere a quack-quack,
An oink-oink here, and an oink-oink there,
Here an oink, there an oink, everywhere an oink-oink,
A moo-moo here and a moo-moo there,
Here a moo, there a moo, everywhere a moo-moo.
Old MacDonald had a farm, E-I-E-I-O.

4. Old MacDonald had a farm, E-I-E-I-O.
And on that farm he had some chickens, E-I-E-I-O.
With a chick-chick here, and a chick-chick there,
Here a chick, there a chick, everywhere a chick-chick,
A quack-quack here, and a quack-quack there,
Here a quack, there a quack, everywhere a quack-quack,
An oink-oink here, and an oink-oink there,
Here an oink, there an oink, everywhere an oink-oink,
A moo-moo here and a moo-moo there,
Here a moo, there a moo, everywhere a moo-moo.
Old MacDonald had a farm, E-I-E-I-O.

5. Old MacDonald had a farm, E-I-E-I-O.
And on that farm he had a donkey, E-I-E-I-O.
With a hee-haw here, and a hee-haw there,
Here a hee, there a haw, everywhere a hee-haw,
A chick-chick here, and a chick-chick there,
Here a chick, there a chick, everywhere a chick-chick,
A quack-quack here, and a quack-quack there,

7. Old MacDonald had a farm, E-I-E-I-O.
And on that farm he had a sheep, E-I-E-I-O.
With a baa-baa here, and a baa-baa there,
Here a baa, there a baa, everywhere a baa-baa,
A neigh-neigh here, and a neigh-neigh there,
Here a neigh, there a neigh, everywhere a neigh-neigh,
A hee-haw here, and a hee-haw there,
Here a hee, there a haw, everywhere a hee-haw,
A chick-chick here, and a chick-chick there,
Here a chick, there a chick, everywhere a chick-chick,
A quack-quack here, and a quack-quack there,
Here a quack, there a quack, everywhere a quack-quack,
An oink-oink here, and an oink-oink there,
Here an oink, there an oink, everywhere an oink-oink,
A moo-moo here and a moo-moo there,
Here a moo, there a moo, everywhere a moo-moo.
Old MacDonald had a farm, E-I-E-I-O.

8. Add your own animals!

About the Song

"Old MacDonald Had a Farm" goes back to the early 1700s, but it has changed over the years. The song came from England, like many other American folk tunes. The people who came from England to settle in the American colonies knew the song.

During World War I, the song was a favorite of U.S. troops fighting in Europe. They found out that the British soldiers knew and liked it, too. At that time, the song was different from the "Old MacDonald" we know today. It was about Old MacDougal's farm in "O-hi-o." By the 1920s, "MacDougal" had changed to "MacDonald," and "O-hi-o" had become the familiar "E-I-E-I-O."

DID YOU KNOW?

The noise on Old MacDonald's farm is very different from the noise on most farms today. Old MacDonald had many kinds of animals. Now, farms usually have only one kind of animal. For example, dairy farms have just cows and hog farms raise only hogs. Wisconsin has more dairy farms than any other state (about 19,000). California has the largest dairy farms. The average dairy farm in California has over 600 cows. Hog farms in the United States and Canada are often even larger. Some have several thousand hogs at a time. One farm in North Carolina has about 68,000 hogs!

23

Make Your Own Barnyard Bandana

WHAT YOU NEED:

- a large white cloth the size of a bandana (perhaps a large cloth napkin)
- permanent markers in different colors

WHAT TO DO:

1. Decorate your barnyard bandana with drawings of Old MacDonald and his farm animals.
2. Hold one corner of your bandana and fold it over to the opposite corner, making a triangle.
3. Put the bandana around your neck and tie the two ends in the front or in the back.
4. Sing "Old MacDonald Had a Farm" while wearing your barnyard bandana.

To Learn More

AT THE LIBRARY

Krull, Kathleen. *Gonna Sing My Head Off!: American Folk Songs for Children.* New York: Alfred A. Knopf, 1992.

Murphy, Andy. *Out and About at the Dairy Farm.* Minneapolis: Picture Window Books, 2003.

Rounds, Glen, Illustrator. *Old MacDonald Had a Farm.* New York: Holiday House, 1989.

Schwartz, Amy. *Old MacDonald.* New York: Scholastic Press, 1999.

Yolen, Jane. *Jane Yolen's Old MacDonald Songbook.* Honesdale, Pa.: Boyds Mills Press, 1994.

ON THE WEB

CHILDREN'S MUSIC WEB
http://www.childrensmusic.org
For resources and links on children's music for kids, parents, educators, and musicians

NATIONAL INSTITUTE OF ENVIRONMENTAL HEALTH SCIENCES KIDS' PAGES: CHILDREN'S SING-ALONG SONGS
http://www.niehs.nih.gov/kids/musicchild.htm
For the music and lyrics to many favorite, traditional children's songs

FACT HOUND
Want more information about traditional songs? FACT HOUND offers a safe, fun way to find Web sites. All of the sites on Fact Hound have been researched by our staff. Simply follow these steps:

1. Visit *http://www.facthound.com.*
2. Enter a search word or 1404801529.
3. Click Fetch It.

Your trusty Fact Hound will fetch the best sites for you!